Contents

Bars 4

Cheesecakes 14

Pies 18

Cakes 25

Cookies 28

Brownies 30

Desserts 34

Candies 40

Beverages 44

Sauce 46

Magic Cookie Bars

½ cup (1 stick) butter or margarine
1½ cups graham cracker crumbs
1 (14-ounce) can EAGLE BRAND® Sweetened Condensed Milk (NOT evaporated milk)
2 cups (12 ounces) semi-sweet chocolate chips
1⅓ cups flaked coconut
1 cup chopped nuts

1. Preheat oven to 350°F (325°F for glass dish). In 13×9-inch baking pan, melt butter in oven.

2. Sprinkle crumbs over butter; pour EAGLE BRAND evenly over crumbs. Layer evenly with remaining ingredients; press down firmly.

3. Bake 25 minutes or until lightly browned. Cool. Chill, if desired. Cut into bars. Store loosely covered at room temperature.

Makes 2 to 3 dozen bars

7-Layer Magic Cookie Bars: Substitute 1 cup (6 ounces) butterscotch-flavored chips for 1 cup semi-sweet chocolate chips. (Peanut butter-flavored chips or white chocolate chips can be substituted for butterscotch-flavored chips.)

Bars

Lemon Crumb Bars

- 1 (18.25-ounce) package lemon or yellow cake mix
- ½ cup (1 stick) butter or margarine, softened
- 1 egg
- 2 cups finely crushed saltine cracker crumbs
- 3 egg yolks
- 1 (14-ounce) can EAGLE BRAND® Sweetened Condensed Milk (NOT evaporated milk)
- ½ cup lemon juice from concentrate

1. Preheat oven to 350°F. Grease 15×10×1-inch baking pan. In large mixing bowl, combine cake mix, butter and 1 egg; mix well. (Mixture will be crumbly.) Stir in cracker crumbs. Reserve 2 cups crumb mixture. Press remaining crumb mixture firmly on bottom of prepared pan. Bake 15 minutes.

2. Meanwhile, in medium mixing bowl, combine egg yolks, EAGLE BRAND and lemon juice; mix well. Spread evenly over baked crust.

3. Top with reserved crumb mixture. Bake 20 minutes or until firm. Cool. Cut into bars. Store covered in refrigerator.

Makes 3 to 4 dozen bars

Bars

S'more Bars

½ cup (1 stick) butter or margarine
1½ cups graham cracker crumbs
1 (14-ounce) can **EAGLE BRAND®** Sweetened Condensed Milk (**NOT** evaporated milk)
1 cup (6 ounces) milk chocolate or semi-sweet chocolate chips
1 cup chopped nuts (optional)
1 cup miniature marshmallows

1. Preheat oven to 350°F (325°F for glass dish). In 13×9-inch baking pan, melt butter in oven.

2. Sprinkle crumbs over butter; pour EAGLE BRAND evenly over crumbs.

3. Sprinkle with chips and, if desired, nuts; press down gently with fork.

4. Bake 25 minutes. Remove from oven; sprinkle with marshmallows. Return to oven. Bake 2 minutes more. Cool. Chill if desired. Cut into bars. Store covered at room temperature.

Makes 2 to 3 dozen bars

Bars

White Chocolate Squares

- 2 cups (12 ounces) white chocolate chips, divided
- ¼ cup (½ stick) butter or margarine
- 1 (14-ounce) can EAGLE BRAND® Sweetened Condensed Milk (NOT evaporated milk)
- 1 egg
- 1 teaspoon vanilla extract
- 2 cups all-purpose flour
- ½ teaspoon baking powder
- 1 cup chopped pecans, toasted
- Powdered sugar

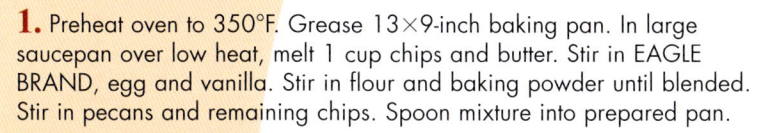

1. Preheat oven to 350°F. Grease 13×9-inch baking pan. In large saucepan over low heat, melt 1 cup chips and butter. Stir in EAGLE BRAND, egg and vanilla. Stir in flour and baking powder until blended. Stir in pecans and remaining chips. Spoon mixture into prepared pan.

2. Bake 20 to 25 minutes. Cool. Sprinkle with powdered sugar; cut into squares. Store covered at room temperature.

Makes 2 dozen bars

Bars

Toffee-Top Cheesecake Bars

1¼ cups all-purpose flour
1 cup powdered sugar
½ cup unsweetened cocoa
¼ teaspoon baking soda
¾ cup (1½ sticks) butter or margarine
1 (8-ounce) package cream cheese, **softened**
1 (14-ounce) can **EAGLE BRAND**® Sweetened Condensed Milk (**NOT evaporated milk**)
2 eggs
1 teaspoon vanilla extract
1½ cups (8-ounce package) English toffee bits, **divided**

1. Preheat oven to 350°F. In medium mixing bowl, combine flour, powdered sugar, cocoa and baking soda; cut in butter until mixture is crumbly. Press firmly on bottom of ungreased 13×9-inch baking pan. Bake 15 minutes.

2. In large mixing bowl, beat cream cheese until fluffy. Add EAGLE BRAND, eggs and vanilla; beat until smooth. Stir in 1 cup English toffee bits. Pour mixture over hot crust. Bake 25 minutes or until set and edges just begin to brown.

3. Remove from oven. Cool 15 minutes. Sprinkle remaining ½ cup English toffee bits evenly over top. Cool completely. Refrigerate several hours or until cold. Store leftovers covered in refrigerator.

Makes about 3 dozen bars

Bars

Fudge-Filled Bars

- 1 (14-ounce) can EAGLE BRAND® Sweetened Condensed Milk (NOT evaporated milk)
- 2 cups (12 ounces) semi-sweet chocolate chips
- 2 tablespoons butter or margarine
- 2 teaspoons vanilla extract
- 2 (18-ounce) packages refrigerated cookie dough (sugar cookie, oatmeal-chocolate chip or chocolate chip dough)

1. Preheat oven to 350°F. In heavy saucepan over medium heat, combine EAGLE BRAND, chips and butter; heat until chips melt, stirring often. Remove from heat; stir in vanilla. Cool 15 minutes.

2. Using floured hands, press 1½ packages of cookie dough into ungreased 15×10×1-inch baking pan. Pour cooled chocolate mixture evenly over dough. Crumble remaining dough over chocolate mixture.

3. Bake 25 to 30 minutes. Cool. Cut into bars. Store covered at room temperature. *Makes 4 dozen bars*

Helpful Hint: If you want to trim the fat in any Eagle Brand recipe, just use Eagle Brand Fat Free or Low Fat Sweetened Condensed Milk instead of the original Eagle Brand.

Bars

Granola Bars

3 cups oats
1 (14-ounce) can EAGLE BRAND® Sweetened Condensed Milk (NOT evaporated milk)
1 cup peanuts
1 cup sunflower seeds
1 cup raisins
½ cup (1 stick) butter or margarine, melted
1½ teaspoons ground cinnamon

1. Preheat oven to 325°F. Line 15×10-inch jelly-roll pan with aluminum foil; grease.

2. In large mixing bowl, combine all ingredients; mix well. Press evenly into prepared pan.

3. Bake 25 to 30 minutes or until golden brown. Cool slightly; remove from pan and peel off foil. Cut into bars. Store loosely covered at room temperature. *Makes 4 dozen bars*

Bars

Chocolate Nut Bars

1¾ cups graham cracker crumbs
½ cup (1 stick) butter or margarine, melted
2 cups (12 ounces) semi-sweet chocolate chips, divided
1 (14-ounce) can EAGLE BRAND® Sweetened Condensed Milk (NOT evaporated milk)
1 teaspoon vanilla extract
1 cup chopped nuts

1. Preheat oven to 375°F. In medium mixing bowl, combine crumbs and butter; press firmly on bottom of ungreased 13×9-inch baking pan. Bake 8 minutes. Reduce oven temperature to 350°F.

2. In small saucepan, melt 1 cup chips with EAGLE BRAND and vanilla. Spread chocolate mixture over prepared crust. Top with remaining 1 cup chips and nuts; press down firmly.

3. Bake 25 to 30 minutes. Cool. Chill, if desired. Cut into bars. Store loosely covered at room temperature.   *Makes 2 to 3 dozen bars*

Bars

Golden Peanut Butter Bars

    2 cups all-purpose flour
    ¾ cup firmly packed light brown sugar
    1 egg, beaten
    ½ cup (1 stick) cold butter or margarine
    1 cup finely chopped peanuts
    1 (14-ounce) can **EAGLE BRAND**® Sweetened Condensed Milk (NOT evaporated milk)
    ½ cup peanut butter
    1 teaspoon vanilla extract

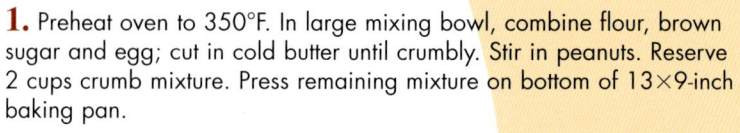

1. Preheat oven to 350°F. In large mixing bowl, combine flour, brown sugar and egg; cut in cold butter until crumbly. Stir in peanuts. Reserve 2 cups crumb mixture. Press remaining mixture on bottom of 13×9-inch baking pan.

2. Bake 15 minutes or until lightly browned.

3. Meanwhile, in another large mixing bowl, beat EAGLE BRAND, peanut butter and vanilla. Spread over prepared crust; top with reserved crumb mixture.

4. Bake an additional 25 minutes or until lightly browned. Cool. Cut into bars. Store covered at room temperature.

Makes 2 to 3 dozen bars

Bars

Festive Cranberry Cheese Squares

- 2 cups all-purpose flour
- 1½ cups oats
- 1 cup (2 sticks) butter or margarine, softened
- ¾ cup plus 1 tablespoon firmly packed light brown sugar, divided
- 1 (8-ounce) package cream cheese, softened
- 1 (14-ounce) can EAGLE BRAND® Sweetened Condensed Milk (NOT evaporated milk)
- ¼ cup lemon juice from concentrate
- 1 (16-ounce) can whole berry cranberry sauce
- 2 tablespoons cornstarch

1. Preheat oven to 350°F. Grease 13×9-inch baking pan. In large mixing bowl, beat flour, oats, butter and ¾ cup brown sugar until crumbly. Reserve 1½ cups crumb mixture. Press remaining crumb mixture firmly on bottom of prepared pan. Bake 15 minutes or until lightly browned.

2. Meanwhile, in medium mixing bowl, beat cream cheese until fluffy. Gradually beat in EAGLE BRAND until smooth; stir in lemon juice. Spread over baked crust. In another medium mixing bowl, combine cranberry sauce, cornstarch and remaining 1 tablespoon brown sugar. Spoon over cheese layer. Top with reserved crumb mixture.

3. Bake 45 minutes or until golden. Cool and cut into bars. Store covered in refrigerator.   *Makes 2 to 3 dozen bars*

Tip: Cut into large squares. Serve warm and top with ice cream.

Bars

Microwave Cheesecake

⅓ cup (⅔ stick) butter or margarine
1¼ cups graham cracker crumbs
¼ cup sugar
2 (8-ounce) packages cream cheese, softened
1 (14-ounce) can EAGLE BRAND® Sweetened Condensed Milk (NOT evaporated milk)
3 eggs
¼ cup lemon juice from concentrate
1 (8-ounce) container sour cream, at room temperature

1. In 10-inch microwave-safe quiche dish or pie plate, melt butter loosely covered at HIGH (100% power) 1 minute. Add crumbs and sugar; press firmly on bottom of dish. Microwave at HIGH (100% power) 1½ minutes, rotating dish once.

2. In 2-quart glass measure, beat cream cheese until fluffy. Gradually beat in EAGLE BRAND until smooth. Add eggs and lemon juice; mix well. Microwave at MEDIUM-HIGH (70% power) 6 to 8 minutes or until hot, stirring every 2 minutes.

3. Pour into prepared crust. Microwave at MEDIUM (50% power) 6 to 8 minutes or until center is set, rotating dish once. Top with sour cream. Cool. Chill 3 hours or until set. Serve or top with fruit, if desired. Store covered in refrigerator.

Makes one 10-inch cheesecake

Cheesecakes

Black Forest Chocolate Cheesecake

  1½ cups chocolate cookie or wafer crumbs
  3 tablespoons butter or margarine, melted
  2 (1-ounce) squares unsweetened chocolate
  1 (14-ounce) can **EAGLE BRAND**® Sweetened Condensed Milk (**NOT** evaporated milk)
  2 (8-ounce) packages cream cheese, softened
  3 eggs
  3 tablespoons cornstarch
  1 teaspoon almond extract
  1 (21-ounce) can cherry pie filling, chilled

1. Preheat oven to 300°F. In small mixing bowl, combine cookie crumbs with butter; press firmly on bottom of 9-inch springform pan.

2. In small saucepan over low heat, melt chocolate with EAGLE BRAND, stirring constantly. Remove from heat.

3. In large mixing bowl, beat cream cheese until fluffy. Gradually add EAGLE BRAND mixture until smooth. Add eggs, cornstarch and almond extract; mix well. Pour into crust.

4. Bake 55 minutes or until center is almost set. Cool. Chill. Top with cherry pie filling before serving. Refrigerate leftovers.

Makes one 9-inch cheesecake

Cheesecakes

Holiday Cheese Tarts

- 1 (8-ounce) package cream cheese, softened
- 1 (14-ounce) can EAGLE BRAND® Sweetened Condensed Milk (NOT evaporated milk)
- ⅓ cup lemon juice from concentrate
- 1 teaspoon vanilla extract
- 2 (4-ounce) packages single-serve graham cracker crumb pie crusts
- Assorted fruit (strawberries, blueberries, bananas, raspberries, orange segments, cherries, kiwi fruit, grapes, pineapple, etc.)
- ¼ cup apple jelly, melted (optional)

1. In medium mixing bowl, beat cream cheese until fluffy. Gradually beat in EAGLE BRAND until smooth. Stir in lemon juice and vanilla.

2. Spoon into crusts. Chill 2 hours or until set. Just before serving, top with fruit; brush with jelly, if desired. Refrigerate leftovers.

Makes 12 tarts

Cheesecakes

Black & White Cheesecake

    2 (3-ounce) packages cream cheese, softened
    1 (14-ounce) can EAGLE BRAND® Sweetened Condensed Milk (NOT evaporated milk)
    1 egg
    1 teaspoon vanilla extract
    1 cup mini chocolate chips, divided
    1 teaspoon all-purpose flour
    1 (6-ounce) chocolate crumb pie crust
    Chocolate Glaze (recipe follows)

1. Preheat oven to 350°F. In medium mixing bowl, beat cream cheese until fluffy. Gradually beat in EAGLE BRAND until smooth. Add egg and vanilla; mix well.

2. In small mixing bowl, toss ½ cup chips with flour to coat; stir into cheese mixture. Pour into crust.

3. Bake 35 minutes or until center springs back when lightly touched. Cool. Prepare Chocolate Glaze and spread over cheesecake. Serve chilled. Store covered in refrigerator.   *Makes 1 cheesecake*

Chocolate Glaze: In small saucepan over low heat, melt remaining ½ cup chips with ¼ cup whipping cream. Cook and stir until thickened and smooth. Use immediately.

Cheesecakes

Key Lime Pie

3 eggs, separated

1 (14-ounce) can EAGLE BRAND® Sweetened Condensed Milk (NOT evaporated milk)

½ cup lime juice from concentrate

2 to 3 drops green food coloring (optional)

1 (9-inch) unbaked pastry shell

½ teaspoon cream of tartar

⅓ cup sugar

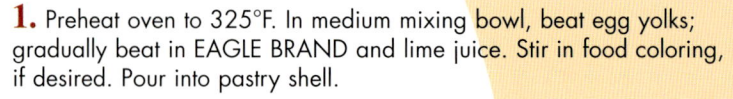

1. Preheat oven to 325°F. In medium mixing bowl, beat egg yolks; gradually beat in EAGLE BRAND and lime juice. Stir in food coloring, if desired. Pour into pastry shell.

2. Bake 30 minutes. Remove from oven. *Increase oven temperature to 350°F.*

3. Meanwhile, for meringue, with clean mixer, beat egg whites and cream of tartar to soft peaks. Gradually beat in sugar, 1 tablespoon at a time. Beat 4 minutes or until stiff, glossy peaks form and sugar is dissolved.

4. Immediately spread meringue over hot pie, carefully sealing to edge of crust to prevent meringue from shrinking. Bake 15 minutes. Cool 1 hour. Chill at least 3 hours. Store covered in refrigerator.

Makes one 9-inch pie

Decadent Brownie Pie

- 1 (9-inch) unbaked pie crust
- 1 cup (6 ounces) semi-sweet chocolate chips
- ¼ cup (½ stick) butter or margarine
- 1 (14-ounce) can **EAGLE BRAND**® Sweetened Condensed Milk (**NOT** evaporated milk)
- ½ cup biscuit baking mix
- 2 eggs
- 1 teaspoon vanilla extract
- 1 cup chopped nuts
- **Vanilla ice cream**

1. Preheat oven to 375°F. Bake pie crust 10 minutes; remove from oven. Reduce oven temperature to 325°F.

2. In small saucepan over low heat, melt chips with butter.

3. In large mixing bowl, beat chocolate mixture with EAGLE BRAND, biscuit mix, eggs and vanilla until smooth. Add nuts. Pour into baked pie crust.

4. Bake 35 to 40 minutes or until center is set. Serve warm or at room temperature with ice cream. Refrigerate leftovers.

Makes one 9-inch pie

Pies

19

Sweet Potato Pecan Pie

1 pound sweet potatoes or yams, cooked and peeled
¼ cup (½ stick) butter or margarine, softened
1 (14-ounce) can EAGLE BRAND® Sweetened Condensed Milk (NOT evaporated milk)
1 egg
1 teaspoon grated orange peel
1 teaspoon ground cinnamon
1 teaspoon vanilla extract
½ teaspoon ground nutmeg
¼ teaspoon salt
1 (6-ounce) graham cracker crumb pie crust
Pecan Topping (recipe follows)

1. Preheat oven to 425°F. In large mixing bowl, beat hot sweet potatoes and butter until smooth. Add EAGLE BRAND and remaining ingredients except crust and Pecan Topping; mix well. Pour into crust.

2. Bake 20 minutes. Meanwhile, prepare Pecan Topping.

3. Remove pie from oven; reduce oven temperature to 350°F. Spoon Pecan Topping over pie.

4. Bake 25 minutes longer or until set. Cool. Serve warm or at room temperature. Garnish with orange zest twist, if desired. Refrigerate leftovers.
Makes 1 pie

Pecan Topping: In small mixing bowl, beat 1 egg, 2 tablespoons firmly packed light brown sugar, 2 tablespoons dark corn syrup, 1 tablespoon melted butter and ½ teaspoon maple flavoring. Stir in 1 cup chopped pecans.

Pies

Cherry-Topped Lemon Cheesecake Pie

- 1 (8-ounce) package cream cheese, softened
- 1 (14-ounce) can EAGLE BRAND® Sweetened Condensed Milk (NOT evaporated milk)
- ⅓ cup lemon juice from concentrate
- 1 teaspoon vanilla extract
- 1 (6-ounce) graham cracker crumb pie crust
- 1 (21-ounce) can cherry pie filling, chilled

1. In large mixing bowl, beat cream cheese until fluffy. Gradually beat in EAGLE BRAND until smooth. Stir in lemon juice and vanilla. Pour into crust. Chill at least 3 hours.

2. To serve, top with cherry pie filling. Store covered in refrigerator.

Makes 1 pie

Note: For a firmer crust, brush crust with beaten egg white; bake in 375°F oven 5 minutes. Cool before pouring filling into crust.

Pies

Traditional Pumpkin Pie

1 (15-ounce) can pumpkin

1 (14-ounce) can **EAGLE BRAND®** Sweetened Condensed Milk (**NOT** evaporated milk)

2 eggs

1 teaspoon ground cinnamon

½ teaspoon salt

½ teaspoon ground ginger

½ teaspoon ground nutmeg

1 (9-inch) unbaked pastry shell

1. Preheat oven to 425°F. In large mixing bowl, combine all ingredients except pastry shell; mix well.

2. Pour into pastry shell. Bake 15 minutes.

3. Reduce oven temperature to 350°F. Continue baking 35 to 40 minutes or until knife inserted 1 inch from edge comes out clean. Cool. Garnish as desired. Store covered in refrigerator.

Makes one 9-inch pie

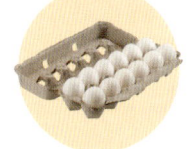

Heavenly Chocolate Mousse Pie

    4 (1-ounce) squares unsweetened chocolate, melted
    1 (14-ounce) can **EAGLE BRAND**® Sweetened Condensed Milk (**NOT** evaporated milk)
1½ teaspoons vanilla extract
    1 cup (½ pint) whipping cream, whipped
    1 (6-ounce) chocolate crumb pie crust

1. In medium mixing bowl, beat melted chocolate with EAGLE BRAND and vanilla until well blended.

2. Chill 15 minutes or until cooled; stir until smooth. Fold in whipped cream.

3. Pour into crust. Chill thoroughly. Garnish as desired. Refrigerate leftovers.

Makes one 9-inch pie

Pies

Peanut Butter Pie

Chocolate Crunch Crust (recipe follows)
1 (8-ounce) package cream cheese, softened
1 (14-ounce) can **EAGLE BRAND®** Sweetened Condensed Milk (**NOT** evaporated milk)
¾ cup creamy peanut butter
2 tablespoons lemon juice from concentrate
1 teaspoon vanilla extract
1 cup whipping cream, whipped *or* 1 (4-ounce) container frozen non-dairy whipped topping, thawed
Chocolate fudge ice cream topping

1. Prepare Chocolate Crunch Crust.

2. In large mixing bowl, beat cream cheese until fluffy. Gradually beat in EAGLE BRAND and peanut butter until smooth. Stir in lemon juice and vanilla. Fold in whipped cream.

3. Spread mixture in crust. Drizzle topping over pie. Refrigerate 4 to 5 hours or until firm. Refrigerate leftovers.   *Makes one 9-inch pie*

Chocolate Crunch Crust: In heavy saucepan over low heat, melt ⅓ cup butter or margarine and 1 cup (6 ounces) semi-sweet chocolate chips. Remove from heat; gently stir in 2½ cups oven-toasted rice cereal until completely coated. Press on bottom and up side to rim of buttered 9-inch pie plate. Chill 30 minutes.

Pies

Rich Caramel Cake

- 1 (14-ounce) package caramels, unwrapped
- ½ cup (1 stick) butter or margarine
- 1 (14-ounce) can **EAGLE BRAND®** Sweetened Condensed Milk (NOT evaporated milk)
- 1 (18.25- or 18.5-ounce) package chocolate cake mix, plus ingredients to prepare mix
- 1 cup coarsely chopped pecans

1. Preheat oven to 350°F. In heavy saucepan over low heat, melt caramels and butter. Remove from heat; add EAGLE BRAND. Mix well. Set aside caramel mixture. Prepare cake mix as package directs.

2. Spread 2 cups cake batter into greased 13×9-inch baking pan; bake 15 minutes. Spread caramel mixture evenly over cake; spread remaining cake batter over caramel mixture. Top with pecans. Return to oven; bake 30 to 35 minutes or until cake springs back when lightly touched. Cool.

Makes one 13×9-inch cake

Cakes

Easy Egg Nog Pound Cake

1 (18.25-ounce) package yellow cake mix
1 (4-serving size) package instant vanilla pudding and pie filling mix
¾ cup BORDEN® Egg Nog
¾ cup vegetable oil
4 eggs
½ teaspoon ground nutmeg
   Powdered sugar (optional)

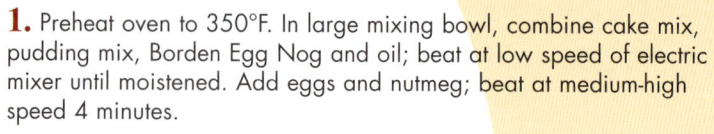

1. Preheat oven to 350°F. In large mixing bowl, combine cake mix, pudding mix, Borden Egg Nog and oil; beat at low speed of electric mixer until moistened. Add eggs and nutmeg; beat at medium-high speed 4 minutes.

2. Pour into greased and floured 10-inch fluted or tube pan.

3. Bake 40 to 45 minutes or until wooden pick inserted near center comes out clean.

4. Cool 10 minutes; remove from pan. Cool completely. Sprinkle with powdered sugar, if desired.

Makes one 10-inch cake

German Chocolate Cake

- 1 (18.25-ounce) package chocolate cake mix
- 1 cup water
- 3 eggs
- ½ cup vegetable oil
- 1 (14-ounce) can EAGLE BRAND® Sweetened Condensed Milk (NOT evaporated milk), divided
- 3 tablespoons butter or margarine
- 1 egg yolk
- ⅓ cup chopped pecans
- ⅓ cup flaked coconut
- 1 teaspoon vanilla extract

1. Preheat oven to 350°F. Grease and flour 13×9-inch baking pan. In large mixing bowl, combine cake mix, water, 3 eggs, oil and ⅓ cup EAGLE BRAND. Beat at low speed of electric mixer until moistened; beat at high speed 2 minutes.

2. Pour into prepared pan. Bake 40 to 45 minutes or until wooden pick inserted near center comes out clean.

3. In small saucepan over medium heat, combine remaining EAGLE BRAND, butter and egg yolk. Cook and stir until thickened, about 6 minutes. Add pecans, coconut and vanilla; spread over warm cake. Store covered in refrigerator.

Makes one 13×9-inch cake

Cakes

Macaroon Kisses

- 1 (14-ounce) can EAGLE BRAND® Sweetened Condensed Milk (NOT evaporated milk)
- 2 teaspoons vanilla extract
- 1 to 1½ teaspoons almond extract
- 2 (7-ounce) packages flaked coconut (5⅓ cups)
- 48 solid milk chocolate candy kisses, stars or drops, unwrapped

1. Preheat oven to 325°F. Line baking sheets with foil; grease and flour foil. Set aside.

2. In large mixing bowl, combine EAGLE BRAND, vanilla and almond extract. Stir in coconut. Drop by rounded teaspoonfuls onto prepared baking sheets; with spoon slightly flatten each mound.

3. Bake 15 to 17 minutes or until golden brown. Remove from oven. Immediately press candy kiss, star or drop in center of each macaroon. Remove from baking sheets; cool on wire racks. Store loosely covered at room temperature.

Makes 4 dozen cookies

Cookies

Chocolate Peanut Butter Chip Cookies

- 8 (1-ounce) squares semi-sweet chocolate
- 3 tablespoons butter or margarine
- 1 (14-ounce) can **EAGLE BRAND**® Sweetened Condensed Milk (**NOT** evaporated milk)
- 2 cups biscuit baking mix
- 1 egg
- 1 teaspoon vanilla extract
- 1 cup (6 ounces) peanut butter-flavored chips

1. Preheat oven to 350°F. In large saucepan over low heat, melt chocolate and butter with EAGLE BRAND; remove from heat. Add baking mix, egg and vanilla; with mixer, beat until smooth and well blended.

2. Let mixture cool to room temperature. Stir in chips. Shape into 1¼-inch balls. Place 2 inches apart on ungreased baking sheets. Bake 6 to 8 minutes or until tops are lightly crusty. Cool. Store tightly covered at room temperature.   *Makes about 4 dozen cookies*

Cookies

Brownie Mint Sundae Squares

1 (21.5- or 23.6-ounce) package fudge brownie mix
¾ cup coarsely chopped walnuts
1 (14-ounce) can EAGLE BRAND® Sweetened Condensed Milk (NOT evaporated milk)
2 teaspoons peppermint extract
Green food coloring (optional)
2 cups (1 pint) whipping cream, whipped
½ cup mini chocolate chips
Chocolate ice cream topping (optional)

1. Line 13×9-inch baking pan with aluminum foil; grease foil. Prepare brownie mix as package directs; stir in walnuts. Spread in prepared pan. Bake as directed. Cool completely.

2. In large mixing bowl, combine EAGLE BRAND, peppermint extract and food coloring, if desired. Fold in whipped cream and chips. Pour over brownie layer; cover.

3. Freeze 6 hours or until firm. To serve, lift brownies from pan with foil; cut into squares. Serve with chocolate ice cream topping, if desired. Freeze leftovers.

Makes about 1 dozen bars

No-Bake Fudgy Brownies

- 1 (14-ounce) can EAGLE BRAND® Sweetened Condensed Milk (NOT evaporated milk)
- 2 (1-ounce) squares unsweetened chocolate, cut up
- 1 teaspoon vanilla extract
- 2 cups plus 2 tablespoons packaged chocolate cookie crumbs, divided
- ¼ cup miniature candy-coated milk chocolate pieces or chopped nuts

1. Grease 8-inch square baking pan or line with foil; set aside.

2. In medium heavy saucepan over low heat, combine EAGLE BRAND and chocolate; cook and stir just until boiling. Reduce heat; cook and stir for 2 to 3 minutes more or until mixture thickens. Remove from heat. Stir in vanilla.

3. Stir in 2 cups cookie crumbs. Spread evenly in prepared pan. Sprinkle with remaining cookie crumbs and chocolate pieces or nuts; press down gently with back of spoon.

4. Cover and chill 4 hours or until firm. Cut into squares. Store covered in refrigerator.   *Makes 2 to 3 dozen bars*

Brownies

Cheesecake-Topped Brownies

1 (21.5- or 23.6-ounce) package fudge brownie mix
1 (8-ounce) package cream cheese, softened
2 tablespoons butter or margarine, softened
1 tablespoon cornstarch
1 (14-ounce) can EAGLE BRAND® Sweetened Condensed Milk (NOT evaporated milk)
1 egg
2 teaspoons vanilla extract
Ready-to-spread chocolate frosting (optional)
Orange peel (optional)

1. Preheat oven to 350°F. Prepare brownie mix as package directs. Spread into well-greased 13×9-inch baking pan.

2. In large mixing bowl, beat cream cheese, butter and cornstarch until fluffy.

3. Gradually beat in EAGLE BRAND. Add egg and vanilla; beat until smooth. Pour cheesecake mixture evenly over brownie batter.

4. Bake 40 to 45 minutes or until top is lightly browned. Cool. Spread with frosting or sprinkle with orange peel, if desired. Cut into bars. Store covered in refrigerator.   *Makes 3 to 3½ dozen brownies*

Brownies

Fudge Topped Brownies

- 2 cups sugar
- 1 cup (2 sticks) butter or margarine, melted
- 1 cup all-purpose flour
- ⅔ cup unsweetened cocoa
- ½ teaspoon baking powder
- 2 eggs
- ½ cup milk
- 3 teaspoons vanilla extract, divided
- 1 cup chopped nuts (optional)
- 2 cups (12 ounces) semi-sweet chocolate chips
- 1 (14-ounce) can EAGLE BRAND® Sweetened Condensed Milk (NOT evaporated milk)
- Dash salt

1. Preheat oven to 350°F. In large mixing bowl, combine sugar, butter, flour, cocoa, baking powder, eggs, milk and 1½ teaspoons vanilla; mix well. Stir in nuts, if desired. Spread in greased 13×9-inch baking pan. Bake 40 minutes or until brownies begin to pull away from sides of pan.

2. Meanwhile, in heavy saucepan over low heat, melt chips with EAGLE BRAND, remaining 1½ teaspoons vanilla and salt. Remove from heat. Immediately spread over hot brownies. Cool. Chill. Cut into bars. Store covered at room temperature.

Makes 3 to 3½ dozen brownies

Brownies

Raspberry Almond Trifles

- 2 cups whipping cream
- ¼ cup plus 1 tablespoon raspberry liqueur or orange juice, divided
- 1 (14-ounce) can EAGLE BRAND® Sweetened Condensed Milk (NOT evaporated milk)
- 2 (3-ounce) packages ladyfingers, separated
- 1 cup seedless raspberry jam
- ½ cup sliced almonds, toasted

1. In large mixing bowl, beat whipping cream and 1 tablespoon liqueur until stiff peaks form. Fold in EAGLE BRAND; set aside.

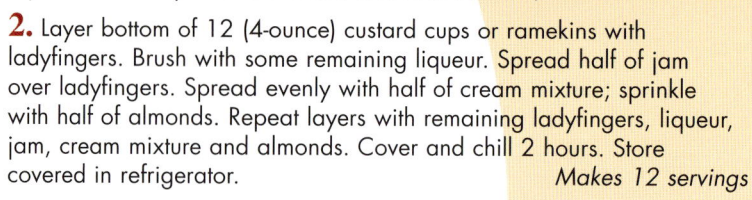

2. Layer bottom of 12 (4-ounce) custard cups or ramekins with ladyfingers. Brush with some remaining liqueur. Spread half of jam over ladyfingers. Spread evenly with half of cream mixture; sprinkle with half of almonds. Repeat layers with remaining ladyfingers, liqueur, jam, cream mixture and almonds. Cover and chill 2 hours. Store covered in refrigerator.

Makes 12 servings

Desserts

Creamy Caramel Flan

¾ cup sugar
4 eggs
1¾ cups water
1 (14-ounce) can **EAGLE BRAND**® Sweetened Condensed Milk (NOT evaporated milk)
1 teaspoon vanilla extract
⅛ teaspoon salt

1. Preheat oven to 350°F. In heavy skillet over medium heat, cook and stir sugar until melted and caramel-colored. Carefully pour into 8 ungreased 6-ounce custard cups, tilting to coat bottoms.

2. In large mixing bowl, beat eggs; stir in water, EAGLE BRAND, vanilla and salt. Pour into prepared custard cups. Set cups in large shallow pan. Fill pan with 1 inch hot water.

3. Bake 25 minutes or until knife inserted near centers comes out clean. Cool. Chill. To serve, invert flans onto individual serving plates. Garnish as desired. Store covered in refrigerator.

Makes 8 servings

Desserts 35

Creamy Banana Pudding

1 (14-ounce) can **EAGLE BRAND®** Sweetened Condensed Milk (**NOT evaporated milk**)

1½ cups cold water

1 (4-serving-size) package instant vanilla pudding and pie filling mix

2 cups (1 pint) whipping cream, whipped

36 vanilla wafers

3 medium bananas, sliced and dipped in lemon juice from concentrate

1. In large mixing bowl, combine EAGLE BRAND and water. Add pudding mix; beat until well blended. Chill 5 minutes.

2. Fold in whipped cream. Spoon 1 cup pudding mixture into 2½-quart glass serving bowl.

3. Top with one-third each of vanilla wafers, bananas and pudding mixture. Repeat layering twice, ending with pudding mixture. Chill. Garnish as desired. Refrigerate leftovers. *Makes 8 to 10 servings*

Desserts

Tiramisu

- 2 tablespoons instant coffee crystals
- ½ cup hot water
- 2 (3-ounce) packages ladyfingers (24), cut crosswise into quarters
- 1 (14-ounce) can EAGLE BRAND® Sweetened Condensed Milk (NOT evaporated milk), divided
- 8 ounces mascarpone or cream cheese, softened
- 2 cups (1 pint) whipping cream, divided
- 1 teaspoon vanilla extract
- 1 cup (6 ounces) miniature semi-sweet chocolate chips, divided
- Grated semi-sweet chocolate and/or strawberries (optional)

1. In small mixing bowl, dissolve coffee crystals in water; set aside 1 tablespoon coffee mixture. Brush remaining coffee mixture on cut sides of ladyfingers; set aside.

2. In large mixing bowl, gradually beat ¾ cup EAGLE BRAND and mascarpone. Add 1¼ cups whipping cream, vanilla and reserved 1 tablespoon coffee mixture; beat until soft peaks form. Fold in half the chips.

3. In heavy saucepan over low heat, melt remaining chips with remaining EAGLE BRAND.

4. Using 8 tall dessert glasses or parfait glasses, layer mascarpone mixture, chocolate mixture and ladyfinger pieces, beginning and ending with mascarpone mixture. Cover and chill at least 4 hours.

5. In medium mixing bowl, beat remaining ¾ cup whipping cream until soft peaks form. To serve, spoon whipped cream over dessert. Garnish as desired. Store covered in refrigerator.

Makes 8 servings

Desserts

Chocolate Ice Cream Cups

2 cups (12 ounces) semi-sweet chocolate chips
1 (14-ounce) can EAGLE BRAND® Sweetened Condensed Milk (NOT evaporated milk)
1 cup finely ground pecans
Ice cream, any flavor

1. In heavy saucepan over low heat, melt chips with EAGLE BRAND; remove from heat. Stir in pecans. In individual paper-lined muffin cups, spread about 2 tablespoons chocolate mixture. With lightly greased spoon, spread chocolate on bottom and up side of each cup.

2. Freeze 2 hours or until firm. Before serving, remove paper liners. Fill chocolate cups with ice cream. Store unfilled cups tightly covered in freezer.   *Makes about 1½ dozen cups*

Note: It is easier to remove the paper liners if the chocolate cups sit at room temperature for about 5 minutes first.

Desserts

Frozen Lemon Squares

1¼ cups graham cracker crumbs
¼ cup sugar
¼ cup (½ stick) butter or margarine, melted
1 (14-ounce) can **EAGLE BRAND®** Sweetened Condensed Milk (**NOT** evaporated milk)
3 egg yolks
½ cup lemon juice from concentrate
Yellow food coloring (optional)
Whipped cream or non-dairy whipped topping

1. Preheat oven to 325°F. In small mixing bowl, combine crumbs, sugar and butter; press firmly on bottom of 8- or 9-inch square pan.

2. In small mixing bowl, beat EAGLE BRAND, egg yolks, lemon juice and food coloring, if desired. Pour into crust.

3. Bake 30 minutes. Cool completely. Top with whipped cream. Freeze 4 hours or until firm. Let stand 10 minutes before serving. Garnish as desired. Freeze leftovers.   *Makes 6 to 9 servings*

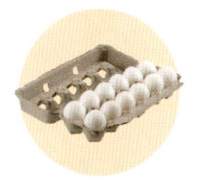

Desserts

Chocolate Truffles

3 cups (18 ounces) semi-sweet chocolate chips
1 (14-ounce) can EAGLE BRAND® Sweetened Condensed Milk (NOT evaporated milk)
1 tablespoon vanilla extract
  Coatings: finely chopped toasted nuts, flaked coconut, chocolate sprinkles, colored sugar, unsweetened cocoa, powdered sugar or colored sprinkles

1. In heavy saucepan over low heat, melt chips with EAGLE BRAND. Remove from heat; stir in vanilla.

2. Chill 2 hours or until firm. Shape into 1-inch balls; roll in desired coating.

3. Chill 1 hour or until firm. Store covered at room temperature.

Makes about 6 dozen truffles

Microwave Directions: In 1-quart glass measure, combine chips and Eagle Brand. Microwave at HIGH (100% power) 3 minutes, stirring after 1½ minutes. Stir until smooth. Proceed as directed above.

Amaretto Truffles: Substitute 3 tablespoons amaretto liqueur and ½ teaspoon almond extract for vanilla. Roll in finely chopped toasted almonds.

Orange Truffles: Substitute 3 tablespoons orange-flavored liqueur for vanilla. Roll in finely chopped toasted almonds mixed with finely grated orange peel.

Candies

White Christmas Jewel Fudge

   3 cups (18 ounces) premium white chocolate chips
   1 (14-ounce) can EAGLE BRAND® Sweetened Condensed Milk
      (NOT evaporated milk)
1½ teaspoons vanilla extract
   ⅛ teaspoon salt
   ½ cup chopped green candied cherries (optional)
   ½ cup chopped red candied cherries (optional)

1. In heavy saucepan over low heat, melt chips with EAGLE BRAND, vanilla and salt. Remove from heat; stir in cherries, if desired. Spread evenly in foil-lined 8- or 9-inch square pan. Chill 2 hours or until firm.

2. Turn fudge onto cutting board; peel off foil and cut into squares. Store covered in refrigerator.   Makes 2¼ pounds fudge

Tip: Fudge makes a great homemade holiday gift!

Candies

Layered Mint Chocolate Fudge

2 cups (12 ounces) semi-sweet chocolate chips

1 (14-ounce) can EAGLE BRAND® Sweetened Condensed Milk (NOT evaporated milk), divided

2 teaspoons vanilla extract

1 cup (6 ounces) premium white chocolate chips *or* 6 ounces white confectionery coating*

1 tablespoon peppermint extract

Few drops green or red food coloring (optional)

*White confectionery coating can be purchased in candy specialty stores.

1. Line 8- or 9-inch square pan with waxed paper. In heavy saucepan over low heat, melt semi-sweet chocolate chips with 1 cup EAGLE BRAND. Stir in vanilla. Spread half the mixture in prepared pan; chill 10 minutes or until firm. Keep remaining chocolate mixture at room temperature.

2. In heavy saucepan over low heat, melt white chocolate chips with remaining EAGLE BRAND. Stir in peppermint extract and food coloring, if desired. Spread over chilled chocolate layer; chill 10 minutes or until firm. Spread reserved chocolate mixture over mint layer. Chill 2 hours or until firm.

3. Turn fudge onto cutting board; peel off paper and cut into squares. Store loosely covered at room temperature.

Makes about 1¾ pounds fudge

Candies

Cookies 'n' Crème Fudge

- **3 (6-ounce) packages white chocolate baking squares**
- **1 (14-ounce) can EAGLE BRAND® Sweetened Condensed Milk (NOT evaporated milk)**
- **⅛ teaspoon salt**
- **2 cups coarsely crushed chocolate crème-filled sandwich cookies (about 20 cookies)**

1. Line 8-inch square baking pan with foil. In heavy saucepan over low heat, melt chocolate with EAGLE BRAND and salt. Remove from heat. Stir in crushed cookies. Spread evenly in prepared pan. Chill 2 hours or until firm.

2. Turn fudge onto cutting board. Peel off foil; cut into squares. Store tightly covered at room temperature.

Makes about 2½ pounds fudge

Candies

Fruit Smoothies

1 (14-ounce) can EAGLE BRAND® Sweetened Condensed Milk (NOT evaporated milk), chilled
1 (8-ounce) carton plain yogurt
1 small banana, cut up
1 cup frozen or fresh whole strawberries
1 (8-ounce) can crushed pineapple packed in juice, chilled
2 tablespoons lemon juice from concentrate
1 cup ice cubes
Additional fresh strawberries (optional)

1. In blender container, combine chilled EAGLE BRAND, yogurt, banana, whole strawberries, pineapple with its juice and lemon juice; cover and blend until smooth.

2. With blender running, gradually add ice cubes, blending until smooth. Garnish with strawberries, if desired. Serve immediately.

Makes 5 servings

Peach Smoothies: Omit strawberries and pineapple. Add 2 cups frozen or fresh sliced peaches. Proceed as directed above.

Key Lime Smoothies: Omit strawberries, pineapple and lemon juice. Add ⅓ cup lime juice from concentrate. Proceed as directed above. Tint with green food coloring, if desired. Garnish with lime slices, if desired.

Beverages

Chocolate Swizzle Nog

- 2 cups milk
- 1 (14-ounce) can EAGLE BRAND® Sweetened Condensed Milk (NOT evaporated milk)
- 2 tablespoons unsweetened cocoa
- ½ teaspoon vanilla or peppermint extract
- Whipped cream or whipped topping

1. In medium saucepan over medium heat, combine milk, EAGLE BRAND and cocoa. Heat through, stirring constantly. Remove from heat; stir in vanilla or peppermint extract.

2. Serve warm in mugs topped with whipped cream. Store covered in refrigerator.

Makes 4 servings

Beverages

Chocolate Peanut Butter Dessert Sauce

2 (1-ounce) squares semi-sweet chocolate, chopped
2 tablespoons creamy peanut butter
1 (14-ounce) can EAGLE BRAND® Sweetened Condensed Milk (NOT evaporated milk)
2 tablespoons milk
1 teaspoon vanilla extract

1. In medium saucepan over medium-low heat, melt chocolate and peanut butter with EAGLE BRAND and milk, stirring constantly.

2. Remove from heat; stir in vanilla. Cool slightly. Serve warm over ice cream, cake or as fruit dipping sauce. Store covered in refrigerator.

Makes about 1½ cups sauce

Sauce